D0537067

ADVENTURES OF KIP

Adventures of Kip

IN ASPEN AND SNOWMASS

BY JILL SHEELEY

ILLUSTRATIONS BY TANYA RICHARDS

COURTNEY PRESS

ISBN 978-0-9795592-2-8

Copyright © 2016 by Jill Sheeley

Published by COURTNEY PRESS · Aspen, Colorado

Even though for the sake of the story Courtney is alone with Kip quite often, we advise children to be accompanied by an adult anytime they're in the backcountry.

Please learn the leash laws in Aspen.

For more information about ordering books write:

Jill Sheeley, PO Box 845, Aspen CO, 81612 · jillsheeleybooks.com

or email at: jillsheeleybooks@gmail.com

Printed by Ingram Spark

DEDICATION

I dedicate this book to
all the wonderful dogs in my life, past and present.
All our dogs have brought so much
joy, love and loyalty to my family and me.
—JILL SHEELEY

I dedicate this story to Courtney, the best
companion and friend a dog could ask for.
—KIP

A very special thanks to
Tanya Richards for making Kip's story come to life;
Hensley Peterson, my editor extraordinaire;
and Marjorie DeLuca, the designing magician.

And to Kip, who provides me with
many amazing moments, adventures and love.

I'm one of the luckiest dogs in the world. I live in Aspen, Colorado. Every day is a total blast.

My name is Kip. I have two blue eyes and very soft fur. People think I'm wearing a coat because I have so many interesting colors and spots. I'm mostly golden brown and white. My ears go flippity floppity when I run. My tongue goes wiggly-waggly. I have two white paws and people think I'm wearing socks.

People are funny!

Let me tell you about a typical day for me in Aspen.

I wake up early and have a hearty doggie breakfast. Then I'm raring to go. I have tons of energy and luckily, my owner Courtney is very sporty so I get lots of exercise. Courtney takes me for super long walks and hikes.

We almost always go into the town of Aspen. As we walk around, I run into many of my people pals and dog pals.

People in Aspen love dogs. Visitors miss their dogs, so I get extra pets.

One of my fun stops—although I have many—is the historic Wheeler Opera House named after a pioneer from the 1800s named Jerome Wheeler.

The Wheeler features concerts, plays and movies. Inside the theater, is a huge chandelier and beautifully painted walls.

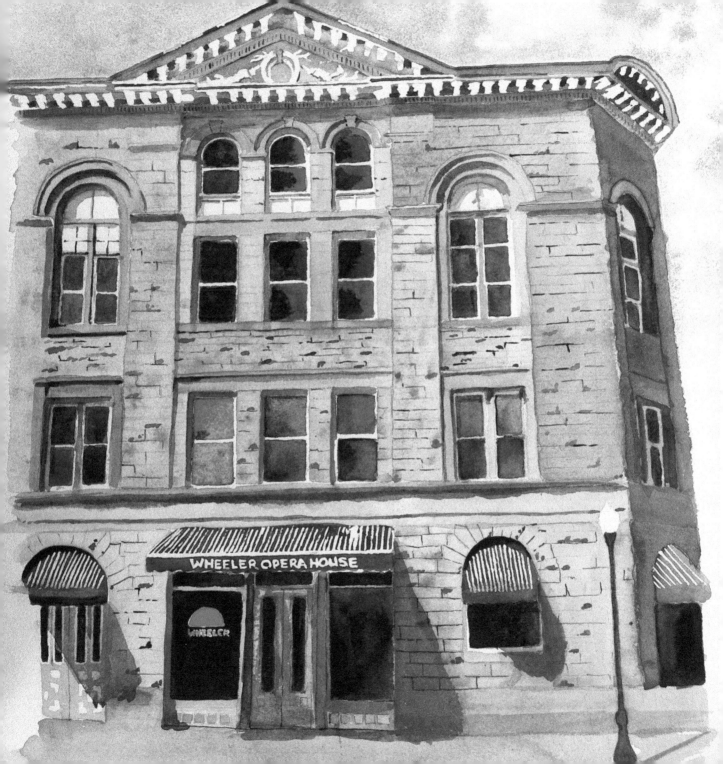

In the Wheeler lobby there are nice ladies who give out information about Aspen and Snowmass. The friendly ladies always give me one or two treats and that makes me happy.

Fall is so pretty in Aspen and Snowmass. The air is crisp and cooler. Even though I have to be on a leash, Courtney takes me up to the world-famous Maroon Bells where we hike along the lake and visit the beaver ponds.

All summer the leaves on the aspen trees are green. But during fall, the green leaves magically turn bright yellow.

Let's say it's a beautiful winter day. Courtney and I can go to either the Aspen or Snowmass golf course. She can cross-country ski and I can run and play with other doggies on the marked dog trails.

We sometimes go up the road to the Pine Creek Cookhouse. Remember, I'm an Australian Shepherd and we need to run a ton.

In January, Aspen has a winter carnival called Wintersköl. It's a week-long celebration with lots of cool things like ice sculptures, ski races, a parade, bag pipers, bands and fireworks.

Saturday is *my* day. It's the Canine Costume Contest, and Courtney dresses me up in a silly costume that fits the Wintersköl theme.

Sometimes when it's really cold out, Courtney takes me to The Little Nell hotel. She drinks hot chocolate and watches the skiers come down Aspen Mountain.

The hotel allows dogs so I come in feeling very special. They offer me fresh water and treats and shower me with lots of attention. They even have pet menus! The carpet is soft for a nap.

Did you know that Aspen was a silver mining town in the 1800s? It's really cool to visit the Smuggler Mine and learn about how the mine worked a long time ago.

Courtney and I hike up the Smuggler Mountain trail almost every day. It's steep and fun and sometimes my brother Ollie comes along.

I love all the seasons in Aspen, but probably my favorite is summer. That's because the days are really long and there are even more things to do.

Courtney and I get up early. She rides her horse Cici and I run alongside to my heart's content. There are beautiful wildflowers to sniff, streams to drink from and new places to discover.

People come to Aspen for fun and culture. After a long run in the mountains, there's nothing better than when Courtney takes me to the Benedict Music Tent. We sit out on the cool grass and listen to the soothing classical music. Did you know dogs love music?

Saturday mornings are fantastic.
From June until October, Courtney and
I stroll around the Farmer's Market.
Colorful fruits and vegetables are plentiful.
Courtney chats with friends and every few
steps, I meet dogs of all shapes and sizes.

People drop all kinds of food items.
I willingly help the clean-up crew.

In the summer the gondola goes up Aspen Mountain. People can hike and eat lunch at the Sundeck. Courtney and I like to hike up the mountain from town, and after lunch we ride the gondola back down. It's fun and the views are beautiful.

My favorite thing
to do is to go camping.
I told you, I really am
the luckiest dog
in the world!
Tune in for my next adventure.

Kip's Scavenger Hunt

Aspen and Snowmass are amazing places!
Follow Kip on his adventures.
We invite you to go on Kip's Scavenger Hunt
while visiting our special area.

Directions

Here are several places or items to find. When you find them, take a photo. If you find them all, email the photos to Kip at jillsheeleybooks@gmail.com. In the subject line, write "Kip" and your name. Kip himself will email you back a certificate!

1. Find one of the bear sculptures on the Snowmass Mall.

2. Find either the Aspen Mountain or Snowmass (Elk Camp) gondola. If they're put away for the season, find either gondola building.

3. Find The Little Nell hotel in Aspen.

4. Find the flag on top of the Elk's Building.

5. Find the Aspen Popcorn Wagon.

6. Find the Wheeler Opera House.

7. Find the Aspen Fire Department.

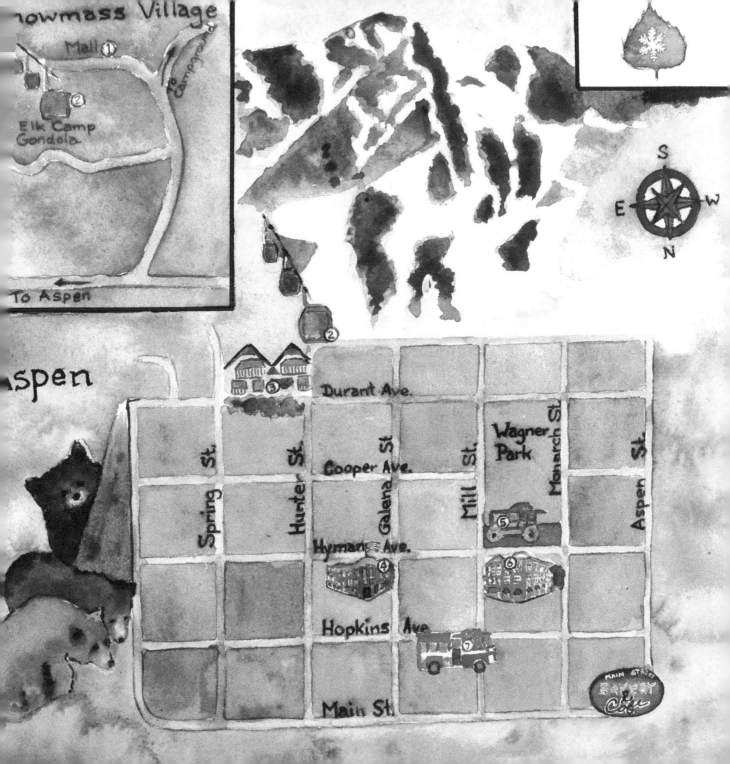

JILL SHEELEY is the author and publisher of eleven previous books. Jill has lived in Aspen, Colorado, for 47 years working at a variety of jobs from ski instructing to hostessing on a mountaintop restaurant and, finally, fulfilling a life-long dream of writing.

Her first book, *Christmas in Aspen* was written as a tribute to the wonderful people of Aspen. Next, she combined her love of cooking with her love of writing, resulting in two cookbooks: *Tastes of Aspen* and *Lighter Tastes of Aspen*.

After having daughter Courtney, Jill embarked on writing and publishing six children's books—*The Adventures of Fraser the Yellow Dog* series, featuring Courtney and their beloved family Labrador, Fraser. Then came *The World According to Fraser*, a memoir written by the now-famous dog. For Fraser fans, she published her first young adult novel, *The Blue Bottle*. Jill teaches writing workshops all around the world and sponsors an annual local writing contest for 3rd and 4th graders.

Jill has been featured on many TV talk shows and radio shows as well as being featured in numerous articles around the world. She speaks to many organizations about her career.

TANYA RICHARDS has had a lifelong love of stories and art. For many years she owned a bookstore in the Canadian Rockies. She is a portrait artist for people and animals and studied illustration at the Academy of Art University. She has recently expanded her art career with a year of studies in art conservation in Florence, Italy. Currently, Tanya lives on Vancouver Island with her two daughters and wide selection of animals.

CPSIA information can be obtained
at www.ICGtesting.com
Printed in the USA
LVHW02*0714040118
561695LV00003B/4/P